D1164888

She's All That!

For all new baby girls—and especially Eve Hélène

KINGFISHER
a Houghton Mifflin Company imprint
222 Berkeley Street
Boston, Massachusetts 02116
www.houghtonmifflinbooks.com

First published in 2006
2 4 6 8 10 9 7 5 3 1

This selection and introduction copyright © Belinda Hollyer 2005
Cover and illustrations copyright © Susan Hellard 2005
The acknowledgments on pages 126–128 constitute an extension
of this copyright page.

The moral right of the compiler and artist has been asserted.

All rights reserved under International and
Pan-American Copyright Conventions

LIBRARY OF CONGRESS CATALOGING-IN-PUBLICATION DATA
has been applied for.

ISBN 0-7534-5852-7
ISBN 978-07534-5852-5

Printed in India
1TR/1105/THOM/PICA(PICA)/120GSMBILTSUP/C

Hollyer, Belinda.
She's all that! : poems
about girls /
2006.

sa   09/25/06

She's All That!

Poems About Girls

Selected by

Belinda Hollyer

Illustrated by

Susan Hellard

KINGFISHER

BOSTON

Contents

Full-o Zest

Best Friends

Sing Daughter Sing

Sweets for My Sweet

Causing a Stir

I Remember You

Growing Up

Introduction

If you asked 100 young women what being a girl is all about, you'd probably get 100 different answers. Being a girl can be a lot of fun, but it can also be challenging and frustrating. Sometimes you might feel that it's all of these at once!

The old nursery rhyme claims that girls are made from sugar and spice, but today's girls add ingredients of their own choosing. You might still find that sugar and spice are part of the recipe—but soccer cleats compete with pink sneakers, and ballet lessons have to make room for science projects. Girls can do and be just about anything they want—and what's more, they know it.

"Girl power" is a great idea, but it's not always easy to feel in control of your own life. There are times when being a girl is just plain confusing. Maybe you have more questions than answers; maybe your life doesn't make as much sense as you'd like; or maybe there's too much space between what you want to be and how you'll get there. It's easy to feel overwhelmed. There are lots of poems that support and encourage girls, and this book is full of them. No matter what you want to do or who you want to be, there's a poem to inspire you and point you in the right direction. There are poems to make you think and to help you sort out your ideas. There are poems to make you smile, just when you need it most.

The girls in these poems dance and sing, play soccer, race down sidewalks, slam doors, and make cymbals bang. They're as sweet as blackberries, they're made of wind and fire, and they weave daisy chains of dreams. They argue and fight; they tell jokes, listen to stories, and make wishes in the moonlight. They look back at how girls used to be and think about the young women they want to become. They can imagine anything—even kissing a frog.

The girls in these poems are all that—and so are you. Whatever interests you most in your life, there's a poem in this book that will speak directly to you. I hope you enjoy looking for it!

Belinda Hollyer

Always Me

What Are Little Girls...

I'm not
a
sugar and spice
girl
an all-things-nice
girl
a do-as-told
good-as-gold
pretty frock
never shock
girl

I'm
a
slugs and snails
girl
a puppy-dogs'-tails
girl
a climbing trees
dirty knees
hole-in-sock
love-to-shock
girl

cricket bats
and big white rats
crested newts
and football boots

that's what
this little girl's

... Made of.

ADRIAN HENRI

They're Calling

They're calling, "Nan,
Come at once."
But I don't answer.
　　　It's not that I don't hear,
　　　I'm very sharp of ear,
But I'm not Nan,
I'm a dancer.

They're calling, "Nan,
Go and wash."
But I don't go yet.
　　　Their voices are quite clear,
　　　I'm humming but I hear,
But I'm not Nan,
I'm a poet.

They're calling, "Nan,
Come to dinner!"
And I stop humming.
　　　I seem to hear them clearer,
　　　Now that dinner's nearer.
Well, just for now I'm Nan,
And I say, "Coming."

FELICE HOLMAN

Girls Can Too

Tony said: "Boys are better!
    They can...

        whack a ball,
        ride a bike with one hand,
        leap off a wall."

I just listened
    and when he was through,
I laughed and said:

        "Oh yeah! Well, girls can, too!"

Then I leaped off the wall,
    and rode away
With *his* 200 baseball cards
I won that day.

LEE BENNETT HOPKINS

I Am Cherry Alive

"I am cherry alive," the little girl sang,
"Each morning I am something new:
I am apple, I am plum, I am just as excited
As the boys who made the Hallowe'en bang:
I am tree, I am cat, I am blossom too:
When I like, if I like, I can be someone new,
Someone very old, a witch in a zoo:
I can be someone else whenever I think who,
And I want to be everything sometimes too:
And the peach has a pit and I know that too,
And I put it in along with everything
To make the grown-ups laugh whenever I sing:
And I sing: It is true; it is untrue;
I know, I know, the true is untrue,
The peach has a pit,
The pit has a peach:
And both may be wrong
When I sing my song,
But don't tell the grown-ups: because it is sad,
And I want them to laugh just like I do
Because they grew up
And forgot what they knew
And they are sure
I will forget it some day too.

They are wrong. They are wrong.
When I sang my song, I knew! I knew!
I am red, I am gold,
I am green, I am blue,
I will always be me,
I will always be new!"

DELMORE SCHWARTZ

When You Call My Name

My Vietnamese name is Ngoc Lien.
My mom says it is a precious stone.
When my teacher says my name
it sounds like she is angry with me about grades.

My Mandarin name is Yu Len.
It sounds so sweet
when my friends call me.
It sounds like, "Come here, I'll give you some candy."

My Cantonese name is Yoc Lien.
It's a kind of flower that grows in lakes with pink color.
When my parents call me
it sounds like, "You have to stay home to do your work."

My English name is Jane.
It sounds like something very strange to me.
When Manh calls, my name is "DE".
In Vietnamese it sounds like "lustful",
so I usually hit him.

JANE DANG

A Girl's Head

(after "A Boy's Head" by Miroslav Holub)

In it there is a dream
that was started
before she was born,

and there is a globe
with hemispheres
which shall be happy.

There is her own spacecraft,
a chosen dress
and pictures of her friends.

There are shining rings
and a maze of mirrors.

There is a diary
for surprise occasions.

There is a horse springing hooves
across the sky.

There is a sea that
tides and swells
and cannot be mapped.

There is untold hope
in that no equation exactly
fits a head.

KATHERINE GALLAGHER

I Am Rose

I am Rose my eyes are blue
I am Rose and who are you?
I am Rose and when I sing
I am Rose like anything.

GERTRUDE STEIN

Today

Today I will not live up to my potential.
Today I will not relate well to my peer group.
Today I will not contribute in class.
      I will not volunteer one thing.
Today I will not strive to do better.
Today I will not achieve or adjust or grow enriched
      or get involved.
I will not put up my hand even if the teacher is wrong
      and I can prove it.

Today I might eat the eraser off my pencil.
I'll look at the clouds.
I'll be late.
I don't think I'll wash.

I need a rest.

JEAN LITTLE

Hanging Fire

I am fourteen
and my skin has betrayed me
the boy I cannot live without
still sucks his thumb
in secret
how come my knees are
always so ashy
what if I die
before morning
and momma's in the bedroom
with the door closed.

I have to learn how to dance
in time for the next party
my room is too small for me
suppose I die before graduation
they will sing sad melodies
but finally
tell the truth about me
There is nothing I want to do
and too much
that has to be done
and momma's in the bedroom
with the door closed.

Nobody even stops to think
about my side of it
I should have been on the Math Team
my marks were better than his
why do I have to be
the one wearing braces
I have nothing to wear tomorrow

will I live long enough
to grow up
and momma's in the bedroom
with the door closed.

AUDRE LORDE

My Life

Look at it coming
down the street
toward us:
it chokes me up
every time I see it
walking along
all by itself.
How does it know
for example
which corner
is the right one
to turn at?
Who tells it
to keep going
past the intersection
and take the first left
after the supermarket?
There it goes –
I'll follow quietly
and see where
it's off to.

JULIE O'CALLAGHAN

Mirror, Mirror

The Mirror

Mirror, mirror, tell me,
Am I pretty or plain?
Or am I downright ugly,
And ugly to remain?

Shall I marry a gentleman?
Shall I marry a clown?
Or shall I marry old Knives and Scissors
Shouting through the town?

ROBERT GRAVES

Who Dat Girl?

Who dat wide-eye likkle girl
Staring out at me?
Wid her hair in beads an' braids
An' skin like ebony?

Who dat girl, her eye dem bright
Like night-time peeny-wallie?
Wid Granny chain dem circle roun'
Her ankle, neck an' knee?

Who dat girl in Mummy's shoes,
Waist tie wid Dad's hankie?
Who dat girl wid teeth like pearl
Who grinning out at me?

Who dat girl? Who dat girl?
Pretty as poetry?
Who dat girl in de lookin'-glass?

Yuh mean dat girl is me?

VALERIE BLOOM

Gloria

Gloria was perfect
In lots of little ways.
She had at least a million friends
And always got straight "A"s.
I think she was the cutest girl
That I have ever met;
The apple of her mother's eye
And every teacher's pet.

But then one day it happened.
The unthinkable, to wit:
Gloria the Perfect
Got a king-sized zit!
Big and red and puffy,
It covered half her brow.
Funny thing about it, though –
I like her better now.

JOYCE ARMOR

Aunt Sponge and Aunt Spiker

"I look and smell," Aunt Sponge declared, "as
    lovely as a rose!
Just feast your eyes upon my face, observe my
    shapely nose!
Behold my heavenly silky locks!
And if I take off both my socks
You'll see my dainty toes."
"But don't forget," Aunt Spiker cried, "how
    much your tummy shows!"

Aunt Sponge went red. Aunt Spiker said, "My
    sweet, you cannot win,
Behold MY gorgeous curvy shape, my teeth, my
    charming grin!
Oh, beauteous me! How I adore
My radiant looks! And please ignore
The pimple on my chin."
"My dear old trout!" Aunt Sponge cried out.
    "You're only bones and skin!"

"Such loveliness as I possess can only truly shine
In Hollywood!" Aunt Sponge declared. "Oh,
    wouldn't that be fine!
I'd capture all the nations' hearts!
They'd give me all the leading parts!
The stars would all resign!"
"I think you'd make," Aunt Spiker said, "a lovely
    Frankenstein."

ROALD DAHL

Lisa

Lisa's father is
Black
And her mother is
White,
And her skin is a
Cinnamon
Delight,
Her hair is
Dark
And her eyes are
Light,
And Lisa is
Lisa,
Day and Night.

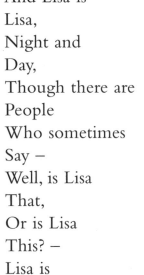

And Lisa is
Lisa,
Night and
Day,
Though there are
People
Who sometimes
Say –
Well, is Lisa
That,
Or is Lisa
This? –
Lisa is
Everything
She is.
Lisa is
Lisa,
Day and
Night,
And her skin is a
Cinnamon
Delight,
And Lisa is
Sun
And Lisa is
Star,
And Lisa is
All
The Dreams that
Are.

BEVERLY McLOUGHLAND

My Sari

Saris hang on the washing line:
a rainbow in our neighbourhood.
This little orange one is mine,
it has a mango leaf design.
I wear it as a Rani would.
It wraps around me like sunshine,
it ripples silky down my spine,
and I stand tall and feel so good.

DEBJANI CHATTERJEE

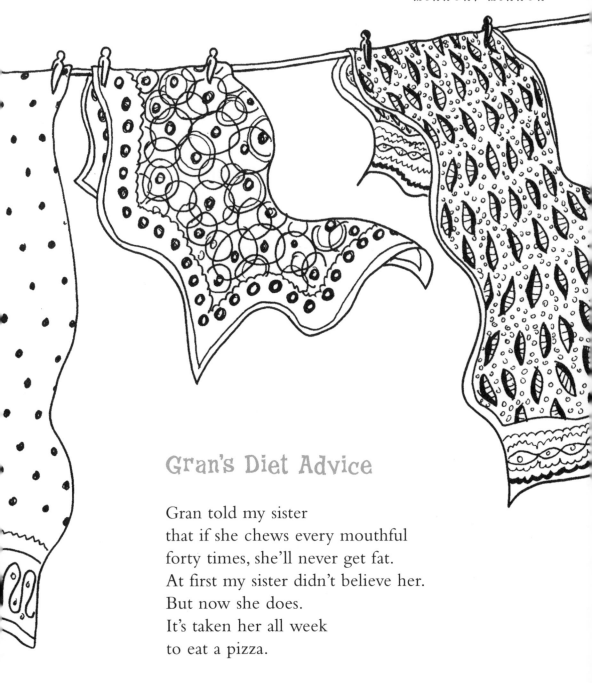

Gran's Diet Advice

Gran told my sister
that if she chews every mouthful
forty times, she'll never get fat.
At first my sister didn't believe her.
But now she does.
It's taken her all week
to eat a pizza.

LINDSAY MACRAE

Purple Shoes

Mum and me had a row yesterday,
a big, exploding
howdareyouspeaktomelikethatI'mofftostayatGran's
kind of row.

It was about shoes.
I'd seen a pair of purple ones at Carter's,
heels not too high, soft suede, silver buckles;
"No," she said.
"Not suitable for school.
I can't afford to buy rubbish."
That's when we had our row.
I went to bed longing for those shoes.
They made footsteps in my mind,
kicking up dance dust;
I wore them in my dreams across a shiny floor,
under flashing coloured lights.
It was ruining my life not to have them.

This morning they were mine.
Mum relented and gave me the money.
I walked out of the store wearing new purple shoes.
I kept seeing myself reflected in shop windows
with purple shoes on,
walking to the bus stop,
walking the whole length of our street
wearing purple shoes.

On Monday I shall go to school in purple shoes.
Mum will say no a thousand furious times
But I don't care.
I'm not going to give in.

IRENE RAWNSLEY

Beauty

Beauty
is a fat black woman
walking the fields
pressing a breezed
hibiscus
to her cheek
while the sun lights up
her feet

Beauty
is a fat black woman
riding the waves
drifting in happy oblivion
while the sea turns back
to hug her shape.

GRACE NICHOLS

Full-o
Zest

The Betsy Street Booters

We are the Betsy Street Booters
We are the girls you can't beat
The sharpest and straightest of shooters
On twenty-two talented feet.

The boys in our school think we're clueless
Which just shows how little they know
We played them last week in the playground
And beat them five times in a row.

The boys say our tactics are rubbish
Soccer skills nought out of ten
We played them once more on a real pitch
And beat them all over again.

The boys in our school blame the weather
The bounce and a bad referee
We played them in glorious sunshine
And hammered them 17-3.

The boys now appear quite disheartened
And wonder just what they should do
They're talking of taking up netball...
But we're pretty good at that too.

We are the Betsy Street Booters
We are the girls you can't beat
The sharpest and straightest of shooters
On twenty-two talented feet.

ALLAN AHLBERG

Esmé on Her Brother's Bicycle

One foot on, one foot pushing, Esmé starting off beside
Wheels too tall to mount astride,
Swings the off leg forward featly,
Clears the high bar nimbly, neatly,
With a concentrated frown,
Bears the upper pedal down
As the lower rises, then
Brings her whole weight round again,
Leaning forward, gripping tight,
With her knuckles showing white,
Down the road goes, fast and small,
Never sitting down at all.

RUSSELL HOBAN

74th Street

Hey, this little kid gets roller skates.
She puts them on,
She stands up and almost
flops over backwards.
She sticks out a foot like
she's going somewhere and
falls down and
smacks her hand. She
grabs hold of a step to get up and
sticks out the other foot and
slides about six inches and
falls and
skins her knee.

And then, you know what?

She brushes off the dirt and the
blood and puts some
spit on it and then
sticks out the other foot

again.

MYRA COHN LIVINGSTON

The Girl Who Makes the Cymbals Bang

I'm the girl who makes the cymbals bang –
It used to be a boy
That got to play them in the past
Which always would annoy

Me quite a bit. Though I complained,
Our teacher Mister Cash
Said, "Sorry, girls don't have the strength
To come up with a crash."

"Oh yeah?" said I. "Please give them here!"
And there and then, I slammed
Together those brass plates so hard
His eardrums traffic-jammed.

He gulped and gaped, and I could tell
His old ideas were bending –
So now me and my cymbals give
Each song a real smash ending.

X. J. KENNEDY

Basketball

When the ball slams hard and heavy
into my hand, and I lift it off
for that layup,
the world shrinks into
one small circle,
and time stops
while I hang in the air.
The net holds nothing but stars
till the ball swishes through
and applause surges in
from the galaxies.
The net fills again with stars.
The whole gym seems full of light.
I feel as if I am shining.

GRACE BUTCHER

Who Is de Girl?

Who is de girl dat kick de ball
then jump for it over de wall

sallyann is a girl so full-o zest
sallyann is a girl dat just can't rest

who is de girl dat pull de hair
of de bully and make him scare

sallyann is a girl so full-o zest
sallyann is a girl dat just can't rest

who is de girl who bruise she knee
when she fall from de mango tree

sallyann is a girl so full-o zest
sallyann is a girl dat just can't rest

who is de girl who set de pace
when boys and girls dem start to race

sallyann is a girl so full-o zest
sallyann is a girl dat just can't rest

JOHN AGARD

The Sidewalk Racer

Skimming
an asphalt sea
I swerve, I curve, I
sway; I speed to whirring
sound an inch above the
ground; I'm the sailor
and the sail, I'm the
driver and the wheel
I'm the one and only
single engine
human auto
mobile.

LILLIAN MORRISON

Double Dutch Girls

Double
        Double
Dutch girls.
        Double
Double
        Dutch.
Our feet
        are fleet
To catch
        the beat.
The street
        we barely
Touch.

We never

trip.

We're hip,

We skip.

All day

We love

to play.

We are

the best.

We'll never

rest

Until

our hair

is gray.

DOUGLAS FLORIAN

Lizzie

Lizzie, Lizzie, spinning top,
Ever dancing, never stop.
Dancing in the morning dew,
Barefoot tap, one two, one two.

Lizzie, Lizzie, spinning top,
Ever dancing, never stop.
Dancing in the sun's warm rays,
Shining brightly at midday.

Lizzie, Lizzie, spinning top,
Ever dancing, never stop.
Dancing as the sun sinks low,
Setting all the lake aglow.

Now she's lying in her bed.
Rosy pillow 'neath her head.
Round the fence a dream comes creeping.
Softly now – for Lizzie's sleeping.

ANONYMOUS (TRADITIONAL POLISH)

Clara Cleech

The poorest juggler ever seen
was clumsy Clara Cleech,
who juggled a bean, a nectarine,
a pumpkin, and a peach.

She juggled a stone, a slide trombone,
a celery stalk, a stick,
a seeded roll, a salad bowl,
a bagel, a boot, a brick.

With relative ease she juggled a
cheese,
she juggled a lock, a lime,
yes, Clara juggled all of these
… but just one at a time.

JACK PRELUTSKY

Track

My track shoes
turn me into a cheetah.
My spikes are claws.
They strike sparks from stones;
they dig into the earth
and secure me to this
spinning planet.
They make me faster
than anyone.
The wind of my own running
puts tears of joy into my eyes.
I am a cheetah
made of wind and fire.

GRACE BUTCHER

Best
Friends

Two Friends

lydia and shirley have
two pierced ears and
two bare ones
five pigtails
two pairs of sneakers
two berets
two smiles
one necklace
one bracelet
lots of stripes and
one good friendship

NIKKI GIOVANNI

Since Hanna Moved Away

The tires on my bike are flat.
The sky is grouchy gray.
At least it sure feels like that
Since Hanna moved away.

Chocolate ice cream tastes like prunes.
December's come to stay.
They've taken back the Mays and Junes
Since Hanna moved away.

Flowers smell like halibut.
Velvet smells like hay.
Every handsome dog's a mutt
Since Hanna moved away.

Nothing's fun to laugh about.
Nothing's fun to play.
They call me, but I won't come out
Since Hanna moved away.

JUDITH VIORST

Best Friends

Sybil says:

If you don't let me ride the bike
    And push the doll's pram –

If you don't let me be the mum
    And you be all the children –

If you don't let me be the queen
    And you be all the peasants –

If you don't let me swing
    And you do all the pushing –

Then I won't like you any more and
    I won't be your friend.

So I say:

… OK – and let her.

Because I couldn't
    Ride and push and swing,
    Be the mummy and the queen
All on my own…
                Could I?

MICK GOWAR

Meanie

Susie boasted she could sing
as sweetly as a bird.

"Yes," I said, "I think you can,
from all that I have heard.

You sing exactly like a crow,
a magpie, or a jay."

And Susie said, "You meanie, you!"
And took her bike away.

AILEEN FISHER

Secrets

Anne told Beth.
And Beth told me.
And I am telling you.
But don't tell Sue –
You know she can't
Keep secrets.

JUDITH VIORST

Best Friends

It's Susan I talk to, not Tracey,
Before that I sat next to Jane;
I used to be best friends with Lynda
But these days I think she's a pain.

Natasha's all right in small doses,
I meet Mandy sometimes in town;
I'm jealous of Annabel's pony
And I don't like Nicola's frown.

I used to go skating with Catherine,
Before that I went there with Ruth;
And Kate's so much better at trampoline:
She's a show-off, to tell you the truth.

I think that I'm going off Susan,
She borrowed my comb yesterday;
I *think* I might sit next to Tracey,
She's my nearly best friend: she's OK.

ADRIAN HENRI

Poem for Two Voices

SPEAKER ONE	SPEAKER TWO
Did you ever have a friend, a very best friend, Who knows exactly how	
	Your sentences will end?
	And the two of you share some goofy, silly jokes
(That don't make any sense to other folks),	
	But both of you start laughing so hard you almost cry, While other people say,
"What's so funny, you guys?"	"What's so funny, you guys?"

SPEAKER ONE

Did you ever have a friend –
you just give her a look,

SPEAKER TWO

And she knows what you are
    thinking like it's written in
    a book.

You say to her, "Remember…?"

And she says, "I totally do."

Did you ever have a friend
    like that?

I do.

Me, too.

CAROL DIGGORY SHIELDS

Perfect Blend

She's a:
Sadness safe-cracker,
A down-in-the-dumps hijacker.
A deepest secret keeper,
A talk-for-hours non-sleeper.
An automatic advice dispenser,
A future candidate for Mensa.
An Olympic-qualifying talker,
A hold-head-high-whatever walker.
A listener to all my woes,
A fear-of-God to all my foes.

A promise fulfiller, gossip killer,
Dance-all-nighter, tiredness fighter,
Solid shoulder for things I've told her.

She's my:
Round the bend, got to spend
Quick to lend, own trend
Perfect blend
Best friend
(what would I do without her?)

ANDREW FUSEK PETERS & POLLY PETERS

Sing Daughter Sing

My Cousin Tiffany

My cousin Tiffany
she's ten too
and tall and tough

When we was littler
we used to fight
all the time

But she would always
beat me up
'cause she was tougher
and stronger

I used to say
it was because she
was a girl
and I didn't want
to hurt her

And she asked me
do I think
girls are weaker
than boys

I thought
and thought
for a real long time
but couldn't answer her back

Besides
she was sitting on me
at the time!

TONY MEDINA

Girls Can We Educate We Dads?

Lisn the male chauvinist in mi dad –
a girl walkin night street mus be bad.
He dohn sey, the world's a free place
for a girl to keep her unmolested space.
Instead he sey – a girl is a girl.

He sey a girl walkin swingin hips about
call boys to look and shout.
He dohn sey, if a girl have style
she wahn to sey, look
I okay from top to foot.
Instead he sey – a girl is a girl.

Listn the male chauvinist in mi dad –
a girl too laughy-laughy look too glad-glad
jus like a girl too looky-looky roun
will get a pretty satan at her side.
He dohn sey – a girl full of go
dohn wahn stifle talent comin on show.
Instead he sey – a girl is a girl.

JAMES BERRY

Mother Knows Best

Vain daughters are told by their mothers
That they're vastly superior to others
     Imagine how bad
     They feel when they hear Dad
Say exactly the same to their brothers.

LINDSAY MACRAE

Conversation

Why are you always tagging on?
You ought to be dressing dolls
Like other sisters.

Dolls! You know I don't like them.
Cold, stiff things lying so still.
Let's go to the woods and climb trees.
The crooked elm is the best.

From the top you can see the river
And the old man hills,
Hump-backed and hungry
As ragged beggars.
In the day they seem small and far away
But at night they crowd closer
And stand like frowning giants.
Come on! What are you waiting FOR?

I have better things to do.

It's wild in the woods today.
Rooks claw the air with their cackling.
The trees creak and sigh.
They say that long ago, slow Sam the woodcutter
Who liked to sleep in the hollow oak,
Was found dead there.

The sighing is his ghost, crying to come back.
Let's go and hear it.

I hate the sound.

You mean you're afraid?

Of course not.
Jim and I are going fishing.

Can I come too?

What do you know about fishing?
You're only a girl.

OLIVE DOVE

When Tonya's Friends Come to Spend the Night

When Tonya's friends come to spend the night
Her mama's more than just polite
She says she's glad they came to call
Tells them that she loves them all
Listens to what they can do
Tells them what she's good at, too
Plays her horn and lets them sing
(Do they make that music swing!)
Feeds them sweet banana bread
Hugs them when it's time for bed
Tonya sure would have a gripe
If she were the jealous type
But she isn't just a guest
She knows her mama loves her best

ELOISE GREENFIELD

Grandma's Child

As far as I'm concerned
The only person
In this world I'm like
Is me. My mom
Says otherwise.
She calls me
Grandma's child. "For starters," she says,
"In stubbornness,
The two of you are twins."
I shrug her comment off.
After all, she's Mom,
So how could she be right?
Grandma Mac and I
Both speak our minds,
It's true,
And maybe we both
Love corn pudding
With a burned crust,
Hate imitation anything,
And believe royal blue
Is, by far, the best
Color in the rainbow.
Okay, so maybe Mom is right.
That doesn't mean
I have to tell her.

NIKKI GRIMES

Daughter of My People, Sing!

sing daughter sing
make a song
and sing
beat out your own rhythms
the rhythms of your life
but make the song soulful
and make life
sing

MICERE GITHAE MUGO

Sweets for My Sweet

Sweets for My Sweet

Not only is she toffee-nosed
But she is… bubblegum-mouthed
      candyfloss-haired
      polomint-eared
      chocolate-button-bellied
      smartie-pantsed
      and liquorice allsorts of things

In fact, she is very, very sweet.

ROGER McGOUGH

Blackberry Sweet

Black girl black girl
lips as curved as cherries
full as grape bunches
sweet as blackberries

Black girl black girl
when you walk you are
magic as a rising bird
or a falling star

Black girl black girl
what's your spell to make
the heart in my breast
jump   stop   shake

DUDLEY RANDALL

How to Get a Girlfriend

First, you have to get to know her.
Then, get her a present.
Don't forget, girls like flowers.
Then tell her all about you
and then ask her,
"Do you want to be my girlfriend?"
If she says "No," don't say nothing,
just walk away.
If she says "Yes,"
don't act silly
because she may think you're stupid
and leave you for another boy.
Don't try to kiss her right away,
and don't talk bad to her.
If you follow my instructions,
you may just get one.

LENIN SALINAS

Boy Girl

Boy	Girl
Garden	Gate
Standing	Kissing
Very	Late
Dad	Comes
Big	Boots
Boy	Runs
Girl	Scoots

ANONYMOUS

Samooreena

When Samooreena went away
Milk turned sour and grass turned grey,
Come home, Samooreena.

When Samooreena went away
Tortoises stayed in all day,
Poets couldn't find one rhyme,
Climbing roses didn't climb,
Come home, Samooreena.

When Samooreena went away
Garden hoses wouldn't play,
Birds, instead of singing, wailed,
Clocks ran down, the harvest failed,
Toast went soggy, soup got lumps,
Maude got measles, I got mumps,
Come home, Samooreena.

Now she's back! Oh Samooreena,
Blades of grass were never greener,
Tortoises stretch out and run
Faster than rabbits in the sun,
Poets cry, "Ah! Spoon and June!"
Climbing roses brush the moon,
Hoses gush and spout and stream,
Toast's like crackling, soup's like cream,
Wheat's all ears, the milk tastes sweet,
Clocks go tick-tock, birds tweet-tweet,
Maude, unmeasled, skips, while I
Mumpless on my soapbox cry,
"Samooreena, Samooreena,
Stay here, Samooreena!"

RICHARD EDWARDS

Miss! Sue Is Kissing

Miss! Sue is kissing
the tadpoles again.
She is, Miss. I did,
I asked her. She said
something about catching
him young. Getting one
her own age. I don't know,
Miss. She keeps whispering,
"Prince, Prince." Isn't that
a dog's name, Miss?

MICHAEL HARRISON

A Bargain

The prince said to the pretty girl,
"I think I'll let you be
My bride, my wife, my helpmate,
If you'll simply agree
To have ten children, mend my socks,
Cook kippers for my tea,
Wash out my dirty underwear,
And never nag at me."

The pretty girl said to the prince,
"You need a wife. I see.
All right, I'll be your partner,
If you'll simply agree
To bring me back last Monday
From the dry part of the sea,
A pair of blue bananas
And a toffee apple tree."

RICHARD EDWARDS

Bertha's Wish

I wish that I didn't have freckles on my face.
I wish that my stomach went in instead of out.
I wish that he would stand on top of the tallest
     building and shout,
"I love you, Amanda."

One more wish: I wish my name was Amanda.

JUDITH VIORST

Old Ballad

Oh, do not marry that wild young man,
      oh, do not marry, my daughter,
or you will live the rest of your days
      on dog biscuits and rainwater.

But marry that wild young man she did,
      glad that he could support her
on the best dog biscuits money could buy
      and the freshest of fresh rainwater.

CHRISTOPHER REID

Juke Box Love Song

I could take the Harlem night
and wrap it around you,
Take the neon lights and make a crown,
Take the Lenox Avenue buses,
Taxis, subways,
And for your love song their rumble down.
Take Harlem's heartbeat,
Make a drumbeat,
Put it on a record, let it whirl,
And while we listen to it play,
Dance with you till day –
Dance with you, my sweet brown Harlem girl.

LANGSTON HUGHES

Causing a Stir

Watching a Dancer

She wears a red costume for her dance.
Her body is trim
and shapely and strong.

Before she begins
she waits composed,
waiting to hear the music start.

The music moves her.
She hears it keenly. The music
pulses her body with its rhythms.

84

It delights her. It haunts her body
into patterns of curves and angles.
She rocks. She spins.

She stretches entranced. She looks
she could swim and could fly.
She would stay airborne from a leap.

Her busy head, arms, legs, all know
she shows how the music looks.
Posture changes and movements are

the language of sounds, that
she and the music use together
and reveal their unfolding story.

JAMES BERRY

Sally

She was a dog-rose kind of girl:
elusive, scattery as petals;
scratchy sometimes, tripping you like briars.
She teased the boys
twisting this way and that, not to be tamed
or taught any more than the wind.
Even in school the word "ought"
had no meaning for Sally.
On dull days
she'd sit quiet as a mole at her desk
delving in thought.
But when the sun called
she was gone, running the blue day down
till the warm hedgerows prickled the dusk
and the moths flickered out.

Her mother scolded; Dad
gave her the hazel-switch,
said her head was stuffed with feathers
and a starling tongue.
But they couldn't take the shine out of her.
Even when it rained
you felt the sun saved under her skin.
She'd a way of escape
laughing at you from the bright end of a tunnel,
leaving you in the dark.

PHOEBE HESKETH

From a Very Little Sphinx

Come along in then, little girl!
Or else stay out!
But in the open door she stands,
And bites her lip and twists her hands,
And stares upon me, trouble-eyed:
"Mother," she says, "I can't decide!
I can't decide!"

EDNA ST. VINCENT MILLAY

Equestrienne
(from A Circus Garland)

See, they are clearing the sawdust course
For the girl in pink on the milk-white horse.
Her spangles twinkle; his pale flanks shine,
Every hair of his tail is fine
And bright as a comet's; his mane blows free,
And she points a toe and bends a knee,
And while his hoofbeats fall like rain
Over and over and over again.
And nothing that moves on land or sea
Will seem so beautiful to me
As the girl in pink on the milk-white horse
Cantering over the sawdust course.

RACHEL FIELD

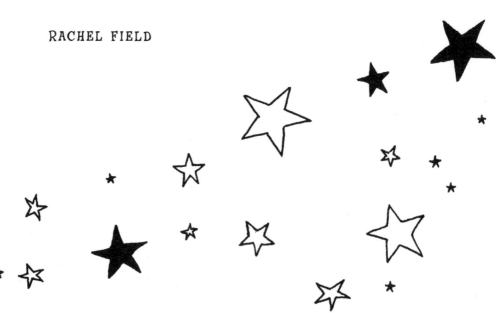

Full Moon

She was wearing the coral taffeta trousers
Someone had brought her from Isfahan,
And the little gold coat with pomegranate blossoms,
And the coral-hafted feather fan;
But she ran down a Kentish lane in the moonlight,
And skipped in the pool of the moon as she ran.

She cared not a rap for all the big planets,
For Betelgeuse or Aldebaran,
And all the big planets cared nothing for her,
That small impertinent charlatan,
As she climbed on a Kentish stile in the moonlight,
And laughed at the sky through the sticks of her fan.

VITA SACKVILLE-WEST

Argumentative

(from Seven Deadly Adjectives)

She'd argue black was white
to be right, that blue was red
to say the last word to be said,
that yellow was green, a king
was really a queen, that bright day
was night.

         She'd have it that
the long was the short of it,
the bottom line was only the tip
of the iceberg and fire was ice, insist
that the hill of a mole in the grass
was a mountain, the spill from a hole

in a glass was a fountain. She'd say
home was away, in out, truth doubt,
reason was madness, goodness badness,
argue the toss till heads were tails, peanuts
were huge rocks, small fry were giant whales
in the churning, quarrelling sea.

CAROL ANN DUFFY

Queen Nefertiti

Spin a coin, spin a coin,
    All fall down;
Queen Nefertiti
    Stalks through town.

Over the pavements
    Her feet go clack
Her legs are tall
    As a chimney stack;

Her fingers flicker
    Like snakes in the air,
The walls split open
    At her green-eyed stare;

Her voice is thin
    As the ghosts of bees;
She will crumble your bones,
    She will make your blood freeze.

Spin a coin, spin a coin,
    All fall down;
Queen Nefertiti
    Stalks through the town.

ANONYMOUS

Rebecca, Who Slammed Doors for Fun and Perished Miserably

A Trick that everyone abhors
In Little Girls is slamming Doors.
A Wealthy Banker's Little Daughter
Who lived in Palace Green, Bayswater
(By name Rebecca Offendort),
Was given to this Furious Sport.

She would deliberately go
And Slam the door like Billy-Ho!
To make her Uncle Jacob start.
She was not really bad at heart,
But only rather rude and wild;
She was an aggravating child.

It happened that a Marble Bust
Of Abraham was standing just
Above the Door this little Lamb
Had carefully prepared to Slam,
And Down it came! It knocked her flat!
It laid her out! She looked like that!

Her Funeral Sermon (which was long
And followed by a Sacred Song)
Mentioned her Virtues, it is true,
But dwelt upon her Vices, too,
And showed the Dreadful End of One
Who goes and slams the Door for Fun.

The children who were brought to hear
The Awful Tale from far and near
Were much impressed, and inly swore
They never more would slam the Door
– As they had often done before.

HILAIRE BELLOC

from The Adventures of Isabel

Isabel met an enormous bear,
Isabel, Isabel, didn't care.
The bear was hungry, the bear was ravenous,
The bear's big mouth was cruel and cavernous.
The bear said, Isabel, glad to meet you,
How do, Isabel, now I'll eat you!
Isabel, Isabel, didn't worry;
Isabel didn't scream or scurry.
She washed her hands and she straightened her hair up,
Then Isabel quietly ate the bear up.

OGDEN NASH

I

Remember

You

Yes, It Was My Grandmother

Yes, it was my grandmother
who trained wild horses for pleasure and pay.
People knew of her, saying:
> She knows how to handle them.
> Horses obey that woman.

She worked,
skirts flying, hair tied securely in the wind and dust.
She rode those animals hard and was thrown,
time and time again.
She worked until they were meek
and wanting to please.
> She came home at dusk,
> tired and dusty,
> smelling of sweat and horses.

She couldn't cook,
my father said smiling,
your grandmother hated to cook.

Oh Grandmother,
who freed me from cooking,
Grandmother, you must have made sure
I met a man who would not share the kitchen.

I am small like you and
do not protect my careless hair
from wind or rain – it tangles often,
Grandma, and it is wild and untrained.

LUCI TAPAHONSO

Aunt Sue's Stories

Aunt Sue has a head full of stories.
Aunt Sue has a whole heart full of stories.
Summer nights on the front porch
Aunt Sue cuddles a brown-faced child to her bosom
And tells him stories.
Black slaves
Working in the hot sun,
And black slaves
Walking in the dewy night,
And black slaves
Singing sorrow songs on the banks of a mighty river
Mingle themselves softly
In the flow of old Aunt Sue's voice,
Mingle themselves softly
In the dark shadows that cross and recross

And the dark-faced child, listening,
Knows that Aunt Sue's stories are real stories.
He knows that Aunt Sue never got her stories
Out of any book at all,
But that they came
Right out of her own life.

The dark-faced child is quiet
Of a summer night
Listening to Aunt Sue's stories.

LANGSTON HUGHES

Girls in a Factory

Seated in rows at the machines
Their heads are bent; the tacking needle
Stitches along the hours, along the seams.

What thoughts follow the needle
Over the fields of cloth,
Stitching into the seams
Perhaps a scarlet thread of love,
A daisy-chain of dreams?

DENIS GLOVER

Woman Work

I've got the children to tend
The clothes to mend
The floor to mop
The food to shop
Then the chicken to fry
The baby to dry
I got company to feed
The garden to weed
I've got the shirts to press
The tots to dress
The cane to be cut
I gotta clean up this hut
Then see about the sick
And the cotton to pick.

Shine on me, sunshine
Rain on me, rain
Fall softly, dewdrops
And cool my brow again.

Storm, blow me from here
With your fiercest wind
Let me float across the sky
'Til I can rest again.
Fall gently, snowflakes
Cover me with white
Cold icy kisses and
Let me rest tonight.

Sun, rain, curving sky
Mountains, oceans, leaf and stone
Star shine, moon glow
You're all that I can call my own.

MAYA ANGELOU

Witch

There was this old lady on the bus...
      (Old cat! Sourpuss!)
Gave her my hand to pull her on.
"OK love... let me help you, Gran."
But she hissed and spat like a real old mog...
Eye of newt and toe of frog.
(She wasn't a bit like my old Nan
Who smells of cake and apple jam.)
If she'd lived two hundred years ago
They'd have ducked her for a witch, you know.

But then I thought...   If her life's
been rough,

                            Why – that's

enough

                            To make her

tough...

                            ... and

spitefulhard.
You can never really tell, you see –
In sixty years that might be me.

MARIAN LINES

Nobody's Nicer

Nobody's nicer
than Mrs. King.

She came to visit
one day in spring,
and let me flash
with her diamond ring.

And even better,
she let me wear
her amber comb
in my yellow hair.

But best of all...
you should have seen!
I tried on her earrings,
and looked sixteen.

AILEEN FISHER

Migratory Birds

ayou were born
to gypsies
though you didn't
want to be
every spring
when orange blossom's
perfume
filled the air
your world was packed
into a few bundles
then your
family was off
living in tents
trailers
dirt floor shacks

you were born
to nomads
though you didn't
want to be
longed to live
with the
settled and the
straight
work in the
five-and-dime
go to school
play tennis
and every time
you found a friend
it was time to go
another town
another round
in a world
that made you
dizzy

you were born
to migrants
though you didn't
want to be
from Texas to
Illinois
living in a blur
out a car window
roads endless
as fields of crops
to be picked by
the piece
never making
enough
to eat
let alone for the
trip back
home
pleading for the
traveling to stop
words in the wind
wooshing by ears
of the gypsy king

you were born
to wanderers
though you didn't
want to be
when you got
the chance
you planted
yourself
deep
in concrete
and steel
to make sure
you or your
offspring
wouldn't
branch out
too far
from home
you were
settled
for
ever

I was born
to a life of never change
though I didn't
want to be
same familiar streets
same people
same stories
year after year
until one sweltering
Chicago summer night
the moon full
color of sun
reflecting off
fields of green
and the sweet scent
of lilacs from
our backyard
helped me sprout wings
so I could fly away.

ODILIA GALVÁN RODRÍGUEZ

Women

They were women then
My mama's generation
Husky of voice – Stout of
Step
With fists as well as
Hands
They battered down
Doors
And ironed
Starched white
Shirts
How they led
Armies
Headragged Generals
Across mined
Fields
Booby-trapped
Ditches
To discover books
Desks
A place for us
How they knew what we
Must know
Without knowing a page
Of it
Themselves.

ALICE WALKER

Girl from a Train

We stopped by a cornfield
Near Shrewsbury
A girl in a sun hat
Smiled at me.

Then I was seven
Now sixty-two
Wherever you are
I remember you.

GARETH OWEN

Growing Up

I Can

I can
be anything
I can
do anything
I can
think
anything
big
or tall
OR
high or low
W I D E
or narrow
fast or slow
because I
CAN
and
I
WANT
TO!

MARI EVANS

When I Grow Up

I want to be an artist, Grandpa –
write and paint, dance and sing.

Be accountant.
Be lawyer.
Make good living,
Buy good food.
Back in China,
in the old days,
everybody
so, so poor.
Eat one chicken,
work all year.

Grandpa, things are different
here.

JANET S. WONG

the drum

daddy says the world is
a drum tight and hard
and i told him
i'm gonna beat
out my own rhythm

NIKKI GIOVANNI

Her Dreams

In her dreams
there are sometimes trees
on which hang ornaments
as tall as she
she lifts her arms
to touch them
if she can stretch
high enough to
claim them
they will become
the jeweled moments
of her life.

ELOISE GREENFIELD

Design

I wanted to organize
my life into
a pattern.

Red socks and
a striped hair bow
on Wednesdays.

For a humdrum Tuesday,
spearmint gum
and a book about horses.

Saturdays, all I'd need
were tassels on my shoes
and a lace butterfly pin.

The way I felt
about Sunday
called for a white

linen dress and straw
hat, a story
about a river adventure.

JULIE O'CALLAGHAN

Little Girl, Be Careful What You Say

Little girl, be careful what you say
when you make talk with words, words —
for words are made of syllables
and syllables, child, are made of air —
and air is so thin — air is the breath of God —
air is finer than fire or mist,
finer than water or moonlight,
finer than spiderwebs in the moon,
finer than water-flowers in the morning:
   and words are strong, too,
   stronger than rocks or steel
stronger than potatoes, corn, fish, cattle,
and soft, too, soft as little pigeon-eggs,
soft as the music of hummingbird wings.
   So, little girl, when you speak greetings,
when you tell jokes, make wishes or prayers,
   be careful, be careless, be careful.
   be what you wish to be.

CARL SANDBURG

Light as a Leaf

Her boat was light as a leaf on her back
as she carried it to the shoreline,

there was grey rising behind the huts —
she'd timed it well, it was dawn.

Her boat was light as a leaf
as she sat, chin on her knees

and the cold tide started to pull
at the frame of her coracle.

She was quick and neat as a fish
as she paddled away out of it,

out of the smoke and the dogs barking,
and a winter of old people dying.

Her boat spun like a leaf
in the rip-tide by the rocks

so by the time the sun came up
she and her coracle were a dot

as she sailed off somewhere
the story can't follow her.

HELEN DUNMORE

Index of First Lines

Index of Poets

Acknowledgments

The publisher would like to thank the copyright holders for permission to reproduce the following copyright material:

John Agard: "Who Is De Girl?" by John Agard from *Get Back Pimple* published by Puffin. Copyright © John Agard. By kind permission of John Agard c/o Caroline Sheldon Literary Agency Ltd. **Allan Ahlberg:** "The Betsy Street Booters" by Allan Ahlberg, from *Friendly Matches* published by Viking 2001. Text © Allan Ahlberg 2001. Illustrations © Fritz Wegner 2001. Reprinted with permission of the author and Penguin Books U.K. **Maya Angelou:** "Woman Work" by Maya Angelou, from *And Still I Rise*, Virago Press. Copyright © 1978 by Maya Angelou. Reprinted by permission of Time Warner Book Group U.K. and Random House Inc. **Joyce Armor:** "Gloria" by Joyce Armor. Copyright © Joyce Armor. Reprinted with kind permission of the author. **Hilaire Belloc:** "Rebecca, Who Slammed Doors for Fun and Perished Miserably" from *Cautionary Verses* by Hilaire Belloc, reprinted by permission of PFD (www.pfd.co.uk) on behalf of The Estate of Hilaire Belloc. Copyright © Estate of Hilaire Belloc 1930. **James Berry:** "Girls Can We Educate We Dads?" from *When I Dance* by James Berry, copyright © James Berry 1988. Reproduced by permission of PFD (www.pfd.co.uk) on behalf of James Berry. "Watching a Dancer" from *Playing a Dazzler* by James Berry. Copyright © James Berry 1996. Reproduced by permission of PFD (www.pfd.co.uk) on behalf of James Berry. **Valerie Bloom:** "Who Dat Girl?" Copyright © Valerie Bloom, from *Let Me Touch the Sky* by Valerie Bloom, published by Macmillan Children's books. Reprinted by permission of Valerie Bloom. **Grace Butcher:** "Basketball" and "Track" by Grace Butcher, from *Girls Got Game* edited by Sue Macy, copyright © 2001 by Grace Butcher. Reprinted by permission of Henry Holt and Company, LLC. **Debjani Chatterjee:** "My Sari" by Debjani Chatterjee, from *Unzip Your Lips: 100 Poems to Read Aloud* chosen by Paul Cookson, Macmillan, 1998. Copyright © Debjani Chatterjee. Reprinted with the kind permission of the author. **Roald Dahl:** "Aunt Sponge and Aunt Spiker" by Roald Dahl, from *James and the Giant Peach* published by Penguin Books. Copyright © 1961 by Roald Dahl, © renewed 1989 by Roald Dahl. Reprinted with permission of David Higham Associates Limited and Alfred A. Knopf, an imprint of Random House Children's Books, a division of Random House Inc. **Jane Dang:** "When You Call My Name" by Jane Dang, from *Believe Me, I Know: Poetry and Photography by WritersCorps Youth* edited by Valerie Chow Bush. Reprinted with kind permission of WritersCorps. **Olive Dove:** "Conversation" by Olive Dove from *Drumming in the Sky*, published by BBC Books. Copyright © 1981 B. D. Bartlett. Reprinted with the kind permission of Ruth Dean. **Carol Ann Duffy:** "Argumentative" from "Seven Deadly Adjectives" by Carol Ann Duffy from *The Good Child's Guide to Rock 'n' Roll* by Carol Ann Duffy, published by Faber and Faber. Reprinted with permission of Faber and Faber Ltd. **Helen Dunmore:** "Light as a Leaf" from *Snollygoster & Other Poems* by Helen Dunmore. Reprinted by permission of A. P. Watt Ltd. on behalf of Helen Dunmore. **Richard Edwards:** "Samooreena" by Richard Edwards from *The House That Caught a Cold* published by Viking 1991. Copyright © Richard Edwards 1991. Reprinted with the kind permission of the author. "A Bargain" by Richard Edwards, from *Teaching the Parrot* by Richard Edwards, published by Faber and Faber 1996. Copyright © Richard Edwards 1996. Reprinted with the kind permission of the author. **Mari Evans:** "I Can" by Mari Evans, from *Singing Black* © 1976 Mari Evans. **Rachel Field:** "Equestrienne" by Rachel Field from *Poems* by Rachel Field. Copyright © 1957 by Macmillan Publishing Company; copyright renewed © 1985 by A. S. Pederson. Reprinted with permission of Simon & Schuster Books for Young Readers, an imprint of Simon & Schuster Children's Publishing Division. **Aileen Fisher:** "Meanie" and "Nobody's Nicer" by Aileen Fisher, from *In One Door and Out the Other* by Aileen Fisher. Copyright © 1969, 1997 Aileen Fisher. Used by permission of Marian Reiner on behalf of the Boulder Public Library Foundation Inc. **Douglas Florian:** "Double Dutch Girls" by Douglas Florian from *Summersaults* published by HarperCollins Children's Books. Reprinted with permission. **Katherine Gallagher:** "A Girl's Head" by Katherine Gallagher, reprinted from *New Oxford Book of Australian Verse*, OUP 1986 © Katherine Gallagher. Reprinted with the kind permission of the author. **Nikki Giovanni:** "Two Friends" and "the drum" by Nikki Giovanni, from *Spin a Soft Black Song* by Nikki Giovanni. Copyright © 1971, 1985 by Nikki Giovanni. Reprinted by permission of Hill and Wang, a division of Farrar, Straus & Giroux, LLC. **Denis Glover:** "Girls in a Factory" by Denis

Glover. Copyright © Denis Glover. Reprinted with permission of the Glover Estate and Pia Glover, the copyright holder. **Mick Gowar:** "Best Friends" by Mick Gowar, from *Third Time Lucky*, Viking 1998 copyright © Mick Gowar 1998. Reprinted with the kind permission of the author. **Robert Graves:** "The Mirror" by Robert Graves, from *Complete Poems in One Volume* published by Carcanet Press Limited. Reprinted with permission of Carcanet Press Ltd. **Eloise Greenfield:** "When Tonya's Friends Come to Spend the Night" from *Night on Neighborhood Street* by Eloise Greenfield, copyright © 1991 by Eloise Greenfield. Used by permission of Dial Books for Young Readers, A Division of Penguin Putnam Young Readers Group. A member of Penguin Group (USA) Inc., 345 Hudson Street, New York, NY 10014. All rights reserved. "Her Dreams" by Eloise Greenfield from *Under the Sunday Tree* by Eloise Greenfield, Harper & Row, 1988. Copyright © Eloise Greenfield 1988. Reprinted by permission of HarperCollins Publishers. **Nikki Grimes:** "Grandma's Child" from *Stepping Out With Grandma Mac* by Nikki Grimes, published by Orchard Books/Scholastic Inc. Copyright © Nikki Grimes 2001. Reprinted with permission of Curtis Brown Ltd, New York, and Scholastic Inc. **Michael Harrison:** "Miss! Sue Is Kissing" by Michael Harrison, from *Junk Mail* published by OUP 1993. © Michael Harrison 1993. **Adrian Henri:** "What Are Little Girls…" by Adrian Henri, from *Robocat* published by Bloomsbury 1998. Reprinted with permission of the publisher. "Best Friends" by Adrian Henri, from *The Phantom Lollipop Lady* published by Methuen Books 1986. Copyright © Adrian Henri 1986. Reprinted by permission of Adrian Henri c/o Rogers, Coleridge & White Ltd., 20 Powis Mews, London, U.K. W11 1JN. **Phoebe Hesketh:** "Sally" by Phoebe Hesketh, from *Song of Sunlight* published by Bodley Head. Used by permission of The Random House Group Limited. **Russell Hoban:** "Esmé on Her Brother's Bicycle" by Russell Hoban, from *The Pedalling Man* published by Heinemann. Copyright © Russell Hoban 1968. Reprinted by permission of David Higham Associates Limited. **Felice Holman:** "They're Calling" by Felice Holman, from *At the Top of My Voice* by Felice Holman. Scribners 1971. Copyright © Felice Holman. Reprinted with the kind permission of the author. **Lee Bennett Hopkins:** "Girls Can Too!" Copyright © 1972 by Lee Bennett Hopkins. First appeared in *Girls Can Too! A Book of Poems* published by Franklin Watts, Inc. Reprinted by permission of Curtis Brown Ltd. New York. **Langston Hughes:** "Juke Box Love Song" and "Aunt Sue's Stories" by Langston Hughes from *The Collected Poems of Langston Hughes* by Langston Hughes. Copyright © 1994 The Estate of Langston Hughes. Used by permission of Alfred A. Knopf, a division of Random House Inc. and David Higham Associates. **X. J. Kennedy:** "The Girl Who Makes the Cymbals Bang" copyright © 1991 by X. J. Kennedy. First appeared in *The Kite That Braved Old Orchard Beach* published by Margaret McElderry Books. Reprinted by permission of Curtis Brown New York. **Marian Lines:** "Witch" by Marian Lines, from *Tower Blocks* published by Watts Publishing. Copyright © Marian Lines. Reprinted with the kind permission of the author. **Jean Little:** "Today" by Jean Little, from *Hey World, Here I Am!* Reprinted with permission of HarperCollins. **Myra Cohn Livingston:** "74th Street" by Myra Cohn Livingston, from *The Malibu and Other Poems* by Myra Cohn Livingston. Copyright © 1972 by Myra Cohn Livingston. Used by permission of Marian Reiner. **Audre Lorde:** "Hanging Fire" from *The Black Unicorn* by Audre Lorde. Copyright © 1978 by Audre Lorde. Used by permission of W. W. Norton & Co. Inc. **Lindsay Macrae:** "Gran's Diet Advice" by Lindsay Macrae, from *How to Avoid Kissing Your Parents in Public* by Lindsay Macrae (Puffin 2000) copyright © Lindsay Macrae 2000. Reprinted with permission of Penguin Group U.K. "Mother Knows Best" by Lindsay Macrae from *How to Make a Snail Fall in Love With You* by Lindsay Macrae (Puffin Fiction 2003) copyright © Lindsay Macrae 2003. Reprinted with permission of Penguin Group U.K. **Roger McGough:** "Sweets for My Sweet" by Roger McGough, from *Pillow Talk* published by Viking—Penguin Books Ltd. Copyright © Roger McGough 1990. Reproduced by permission of PFD (www.pfd.co.uk) on behalf of Roger McGough. **Beverly McLoughland:** "Lisa" by Beverly McLoughland, from *Through Our Eyes—Poems and Pictures About Growing Up* edited by Lee Bennett Hopkins, Little Brown & Company 1992. Used by permission of the author, who controls all the rights. **Tony Medina:** "My Cousin Tiffany" by Tony Medina, from *Deshawn Days*, text copyright © 2001 by Tony Medina. Permission arranged with Lee & Low Books Inc., New York, NY 10016. **Edna St. Vincent Millay:** "From a Very Little Sphinx" by Edna St. Vincent Millay, from *Selected Poems* published by Carcanet Press. Reprinted with permission of the publishers. **Lillian Morrison:** "The Sidewalk Racer" by Lillian Morrison, from *The Sidewalk Racer and Other Poems of Sports and Motion* by Lillian Morrison, © 1965, 1967, 1968,1977 by Lillian Morrison. Used by permission of Marian Reiner for the

author. **Micere Githae Mugo:** "Daughter of My People, Sing!" by Micere Githae Mugo, from *Is That the New Moon?* edited by Wendy Cope, published by HarperCollins 1989. Reprinted with the kind permission of the author. **Ogden Nash:** "The Adventures of Isabel" by Ogden Nash from *Many Long Years Ago.* Copyright © 1936 by Ogden Nash, renewed. Reprinted by permission of Curtis Brown Ltd. and Andre Deutsch U.K. **Grace Nichols:** "Beauty" by Grace Nichols from *The Fat Black Woman's Poems* published by Virago © Grace Nicholl 1984. Reprinted with permission of Curtis Brown U.K. **Julie O'Callaghan:** "My Life" and "Design" by Julie O'Callaghan, from *Two Barks*, published by Bloodaxe Books 1998. Reprinted with permission of Bloodaxe Books Limited. **Gareth Owen:** "Girl from a Train" by Gareth Owen, from *Collected Poems for Children* published by Macmillan Children's Books. Copyright © Gareth Owen 2000. Reprinted with permission of Gareth Owen c/o Rogers, Coleridge & White Ltd., 20 Powis Mews, London, U.K. W11 1JN. **Andrew Fusek Peters and Polly Peters:** "Perfect Blend" by Andrew Fusek Peters and Polly Peters, from *Poems with Attitude*, Hodder Wayland 2002. Copyright © 2000 Andrew Fusek Peters and Polly Peters. Reprinted with permission of Hodder & Stoughton Publishers. **Jack Prelutsky:** "Clara Cleech" by Jack Prelutsky from *It's Raining Pigs and Noodles* by Jack Prelutsky. Copyright © 2000 by Jack Prelutsky. Used by permission of HarperCollins Publishers. **Dudley Randall:** "Blackberry Sweet" by Dudley Randall, from *Knock at a Star,* Little Brown 1999. Reprinted with permission of the Dudley Randall Estate. **Irene Rawnsley:** "Purple Shoes" by Irene Rawnsley, from *All in the Family* edited by John Foster and published by OUP. © Irene Rawnsley 1993. Reprinted with the kind permission of the author. **Christopher Reid:** "Old Ballad" by Christopher Reid, copyright © Christopher Reid. Reprinted with permission of Ondt & Gracehoper. **Odilia Galván Rodríguez:** "Migratory Birds" by Odilia Galván Rodríguez. Copyright © Odilia Galván Rodríguez. Reprinted with the kind permission of the author. **Vita Sackville-West:** "Full Moon" by Vita Sackville-West from *Collected Poems: Volume 1.* Copyright © Vita Sackville-West 1933. Reproduced with permission of Curtis Brown Group Ltd. London on behalf of the Estate of Vita Sackville-West. **Lenin Salinas:** "How to Get a Girlfriend" by Lenin Salinas, from *Believe Me, I Know: Poetry and Photography by WritersCorps Youth* edited by Valerie Chow Bush. Reprinted with permissions of WritersCorps. **Carl Sandburg:** "Little Girl, Be Careful What You Say" from *The Complete Poems of Carl Sandburg* Copyright © 1950 by Carl Sandburg and renewed 1978 by Margaret Sandburg, Helga Sandburg Crile, and Janet Sandburg. Reprinted with permission of Harcourt Inc. **Delmore Schwartz:** "I Am Cherry Alive" by Delmore Schwartz from *Summer Knowledge, New and Selected Poems* published by Doubleday. **Carol Diggory Shields:** "Poem for Two Voices" by Carol Diggory Shields, from *Almost Too Late to School* published by Dutton Children's Books. **Gertrude Stein:** "I Am Rose" by Gertrude Stein, from *The World Is Round.* Published by Addison Wesley Co. Inc. Copyright © Gertrude Stein, 1939, renewed 1967 by Daniel C. Joseph. Reprinted with permission of David Higham Associates Limited and Levin & Gann on behalf of The Estate of Gertrude Stein, through Literary Executor Mr. Standford Gann. **Luci Tapahonso:** "Yes, It Was My Grandmother" by Luci Tapahonso, from *A Breeze Swept Through* published by West End Press, 1987. **Judith Viorst:** "Bertha's Wish," "Secrets," and "Since Hanna Moved Away" by Judith Viorst, from *If I Were in Charge of the World and Other Worries* by Judith Viorst, text © 1981 Judith Viorst. Reprinted with the permission of Atheneum Books for Young Readers, an imprint of Simon & Schuster Children's Publishing and by permission of Lescher & Lescher Ltd. **Alice Walker:** "Women" by Alice Walker, from *Revolutionary Petunias* published by Orion. Reprinted with permission of David Higham Associates Limited. **Janet S. Wong:** "When I Grow Up" by Janet S. Wong, from *A Suitcase of Seaweed* published by Margaret McElderry Books, 1996. © Janet Wong, 1996. Reprinted with permission of Simon & Schuster Inc.

Every effort has been made to obtain permission to reproduce copyright material, but there may have been cases where we have been unable to trace a copyright holder. The publisher would be happy to correct any omissions in future printings.